THREAD PAINTING

A Workshop

with
EVE BOTELHO

FREE MOTION EMBROIDERY TECHNIQUES

For my husband and two daughters

© Eve Botelho, 2014
All rights reserved
Printed in the United States of America
ISBN: 978-0-578-14091-9
www.evebotelho.com

Design and layout: Denison Creative, Rochester NY
Photographers:
Stephanie Quinones Millet
Alene Pierro
Denise Kovnat
Eve Botelho

Cover art: *Eve Botelho,* TREE IN HIGHLAND PARK

Eve Botelho creates Embroidered landscapes with thread, dyes, fabric and a sewing machine. Using a variety of influences, memories, sketches and photographs she interprets her love of the countryside and gardens into thread paintings. She sells her work through galleries and craft shows and teaches workshops. Eve's early exposure to the creative possibilities of fiber was her grandmother who made a living as a milliner and tailor. She spent many childhood days experimenting with the threads and fabrics she found in her grandmother's home. After completing an art foundation course at Mansfield College of Art, where she had the opportunity to work with other media such as painting, printing, ceramics, weaving and sculpture, she completed a degree in fine art and textiles with a focus on embroidery at Loughborough College in Leicestershire, England.

Eve Botelho, FORMAL GARDEN
Opposite page: DETAIL

Table of Contents

INTRODUCTION	5
MATERIALS	6
INTUITIVE DESIGN	8
DESIGN FOR THE PROJECT	10
AIRBRUSHING	12
EXERCISE ONE	15
EXERCISE TWO	16
EXERCISE THREE	16
BEGINNING FREE-MOTION EMBROIDERY	18
BEGINNING THE FIRST PROJECT	26
SECOND PROJECT, AUTUMN TREES	32
THIRD PROJECT, A FIELD IN MENDON	41
FOURTH PROJECT, GOLDENRODS	43
CONCLUSION, PRESENTATION	47

Eve Botelho
LILACS AND AZALEAS IN HIGHLAND PARK
Above, source photograph
Below, left, enlarged detail showing stitches

Introduction

Thread painting is an art form that has really evolved and developed over the last few years. Beginning as an amalgamation of two disciplines, painting and machine embroidery, it has flourished as more artists have begun to explore its versatility, experimenting with different techniques and adapting it to their own styles.

Thread painting is a technique that lends itself particularly well to translating landscapes and the delicate textures, patterns, and lines we find in nature. Both the sheen of the thread and the direction of the stitchery allow the artist to create interesting and beautiful texture that sometimes seems to mimic Pointillism. As the artist becomes more skillful and gains a degree of confidence with machine embroidery, work can be accomplished with both precision and speed.

I was first introduced to machine embroidery while I was in college studying textile design. I soon discovered how versatile it is and what fun it could be. I think it is worth mentioning, though, that it did take some persistence before I felt completely comfortable. I would encourage anyone who is drawn to the medium, but feels a little intimidated by it, not to give up but to have fun experimenting.

When I first began to use the sewing machine to do free-motion embroidery, I used it primarily to create decorative design samples for bed linens and items of fashion, using the techniques of cut work, lace work and applique. It was not until I left college and moved to the United States that I began to adapt the techniques I had learned to create small landscapes. The landscapes of my home in England were my initial source of inspiration, particularly the gardens and the patchwork landscapes and rolling hills of Sussex. I taught workshops – such as surface-design techniques, fabric manipulation, and machine-embroidery techniques – to adults in evening classes and to fiber enthusiasts. It was during this time that that my students encouraged me to sell my work. Since then I have been selling my work at arts and craft shows and galleries and teaching workshops when time has allowed. These days, I find my inspiration in the landscapes and farmlands near my home in Upstate New York.

This book is the result of the workshops I have led and many years of creating thread paintings. It is written as a step-by-step process, showing you how I might proceed as I create a thread-painted landscape. It is intended as an introduction to the method and potential of thread painting. It will guide you through the practical and creative stages.

It begins with outlining the materials needed and how to paint backgrounds onto silk, guides you through the design process, and demonstrates beginning free-motion embroidery and how to begin your thread painting using three stitches with your sewing machine. I hope you will find these workshops both helpful and inspirational.

Materials

Sewing Machine, suitable for free-motion embroidery.

Threads (I use DMC embroidery threads because they have a lovely sheen)

Embroidery scissors

Embroidery hoops

Silk fabric

White cotton fabric

Camera

Light box (optional)

Sketch pad and pencil

Tracing paper

Blotting paper (to make a stencil)

Exacto knife

Quilting cutting board

Wooden stretching frames (to stretch silk for painting)

Silk thumb tacks

Dyes

Mixing tray

Paint brushes

Air brush

Compressor for the airbrush

Masking tape

Small screw drivers

There are as many ways to approach design as there are designers. In this book I will show you how I begin and then proceed to working on and finishing a thread painting. Ultimately the goal of this book is to help you find your own path, whether you are a quilter, a painter, or a fiber enthusiast. It is my hope that these workshops will be the beginning of a new adventure or as an adjunct for the more experienced fiber enthusiast. If you are an experienced artist you will have little need for guidance in this area.

This section is intended for those with little experience with drawing or design. There are specific ways to begin a project. It often seems that getting started is the most difficult part of the design process, but it doesn't have to be. I encourage you to look for inspiration in all places. Once you begin to really observe everything around you, you will find a wealth of amazing subjects.

These particular workshops will focus on landscapes. I suggest that you take as many photographs of places you love or that you can see being of interest to you. Keep a sketch book: it is helpful. Through drawing we begin to really "see" and, as we learn to see, our drawing improves.

The very idea of creating a design can seem daunting to many people, but learning to really notice what is around you is actually the essence of all design. To avoid a broad and directionless search for inspiration, you can think

Here is an example of two different views of the same tree.

Combining these two views I created the design for the Thread Painting on the cover of the book.

Sketchbooks of ideas.

Intuitive Design

about the sort of image you would really enjoy making. As you begin look around you, notice color, shapes, patterns, light, and darkness. Ask yourself, are there particular colors that attract you? What kind of landscapes do you love? Are they wide-open spaces or are they full of foliage? Are they intimate gardens? Begin by noticing an area of your garden, for example, and how the sunlight casts shadows on the lawn. When you are out for a drive or a walk notice the shape of trees or the beautiful color of the sky. Once you start to observe color and shape and details you can begin to translate these elements into a design.

Color is an important element in any creation and nature is our greatest teacher. Nature provides us with an unlimited palette to work from, with fabulous color combinations. Color can elicit an immediate response and elevate a mood. By observing nature you will be able to obtain realistic results. Study the shape and color of a leaf or a butterfly wing.

As I mentioned, some of you may be experienced artists, while others are just beginning. Start where you are. Just be assured if you are a beginner that you will still be able to create your own designs and accomplish a thread painting after a little practice. Keep it simple initially; enthusiasm is important.

Collected photos of Landscapes.

While acknowledging that there are many ways to approach design, for the purpose of this workshop I am going to demonstrate in this book two fairly simple ways to begin. Using favorite photographs of landscapes, garden scenes, plants, and flowers, we will translate these into a thread painting. The photographs often have a color range within them that you can choose to work from. For example, autumn scenes have reds, rusts, greens, yellows, and oranges. A spring day will have bright greens, yellows, whites, and, of course, the colors of spring flowers. A rainy day will have softer, duller greens and grays.

Color choices based on the photograph of Lilacs in the Park.

Mat board corners.

The next step, once a photograph has been chosen, is to enlarge it in the printer and print out one or two copies. Then, using two corners of a mat board, move them around over the print until you find a section or sections of the photograph that interest you and that seem to work. These two corners create a frame.

The mat boards are moved to show different perspective.

Design for the Project

Corners of Mat board show different views of the source photograph.

You may change the size of the frame with these two corners by moving them closer together and further apart. I find this helps me to see the same view from a different vantage point and focus on certain areas. By narrowing the view, it helps us notice different shapes and areas of interest. This approach allows you to view the scene from a different perspective. The frame allows you to have trees or shrubs placed in different areas of the picture. You can alter where your horizon is placed in the picture and so on. Do you want your trees off to one side, for example? Another way to create the design from the photograph is to make a simple line drawing from it and enlarge it in a printer. If you are happy with the photo as it is, it is ready to be transferred onto tracing paper.

Before you settle on a particular design, it is a good idea to think about whether or not the chosen subject is within your capabilities. If it has a great amount of detail in it and you are a beginner, you may be disappointed with the results and become discouraged. So, if you are a beginner, keep it simple.

There are many ways to create a background for your embroidery and I have experimented with a few different techniques. In this book I will cover airbrushing. Airbrushing has two main advantages over other painting techniques. The artist can produce a broad area or a fine line, depending on the height of the airbrush from the surface. This requires some initial experimenting before you begin your thread painting.

PREPARING THE BACKGROUND FOR STITCHING

Airbrushing is a skill which, like any skill, must be applied to the artist's own creative aims. It can be used to render highly finished, realistic images and it can be used simply to fill in a traced image. But, however it is used, there are certain basic techniques that must be learned and understood.

I use airbrushing to create a soft background, sometimes a mere wash of color.

When I need more defined lines I use stencils that I have created.

The details of the painting are created with the thread. The technique of airbrushing will be covered fairly briefly in this book, showing you how to create the effects needed for these particular projects.

Air Brushing

There are a variety of different kinds of airbrushes. I use an Iwata Eclipse. This has a small well on the side of the brush for the dyes. The amount of dye or paint that the small well can hold is sufficient for the small landscapes. If you are going to create a larger piece, use an air brush with a bottle attached.

You will need an air compressor. I use an Iwata Studio Series compressor, as it is nice and quiet when it is running.

BEFORE BEGINNING to airbrush onto your silk, it will be necessary to practice with your airbrush on paper or on some inexpensive calico cotton. You will need to learn to master control of the lever action of the airbrush itself. Do not feel intimidated; you will soon get the feeling for the amount of pressure needed to create certain marks. I bought my airbrush and then took a couple of evening classes, but you may not find this necessary as you can now go online and watch a video about airbrushing. You may also watch the video on my website.

Make sure you wear a face mask. Some of the dyes and paints can be toxic when used in quantity. Also, work in a well-ventilated room. However, this process is used fairly briefly for the projects in this book. If you find you really like the effects created with the airbrush and would like to do more with it, books on just this topic are available. It may seem messy and awkward at first and I have spilled the dyes many times, so having the floors covered is a good idea too. Or have plenty of rags or paper towels on hand.

GATHER all your equipment together for the airbrushing.

ATTACH the hose to the air compressor.

FILL the well or the bottle on the air brush with small amounts of paints or dyes.

THE NEXT ESSENTIAL THING is to find a comfortable steady way of holding the airbrush and manipulating the finger-control lever. There are no fixed rules; it is just a matter of experimenting. The airbrush is balanced in the curve of the hand between thumb and forefinger, supported between the thumb and middle finger and leaving the forefinger free to manipulate the lever control. You can see in the pictures how to hold the airbrush.

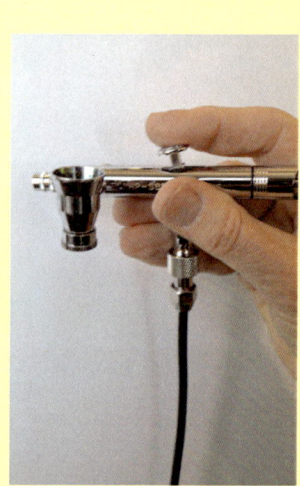

FIGURE 1
Hold the airbrush as you would a pen, with the thumb and middle finger supporting it underneath. To release the air flow, press down on the button with the index finger.

FIGURE 2
To release paint, pull back the button while keeping it depressed. Then pull back the lever and press down. The amount of pressure and the distance the airbrush is from the fabric, the narrower or wider the stroke. This may feel awkward at first, but soon you will have a sense of how hard to push down on the lever as you pull it back.

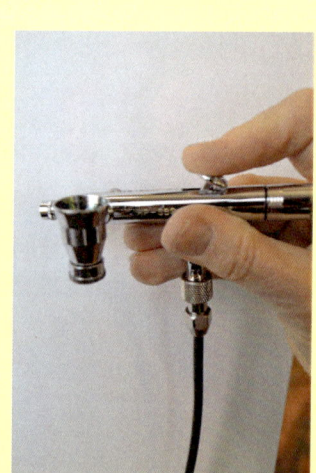

FIGURE 3
For a smooth effect, it is important to stop the paint flow before stopping the air flow, so ease the button back to its original position.

Air Brushing, continued

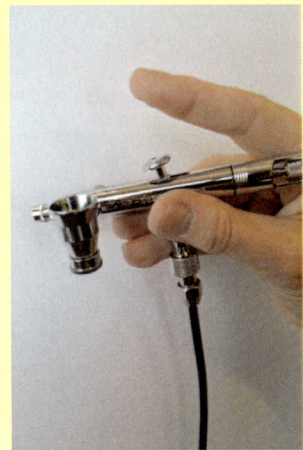

FIGURE 4
Stop the air flow by lifting the index finger from the button, releasing the pressure on the button.

Exercise One

THE FIRST STEP in beginning to learn about gaining control of the airbrush is to practice "line ruling."

Against a wall or on your easel, set up some paper or some fabric that has been stretched onto a frame. Make sure that there is something behind the paper in case you have any mishaps: you don't want to spray furnishings or your walls. Cut a straight piece of card or use a ruler and run the airbrush along the side of the ruler or card.

Holding the airbrush at an angle, first hold it close to the ruler or card, pull the lever back, and begin to spray and move the airbrush along the edge. Then, move the ruler or card half an inch over and run the airbrush along the edge – but this time hold the airbrush farther away. You will see that the area of dye or paint becomes wider as the distance becomes greater.

Do this several times, moving the card a little each time. First do it vertically, then make horizontal marks. Practice moving the lever backwards and forwards while putting different amounts of pressure on it. Notice the difference in density and width.

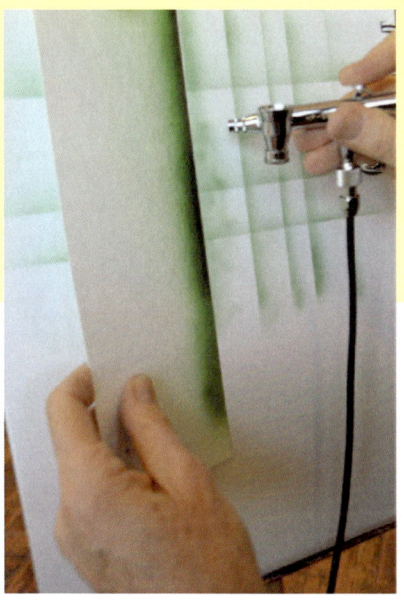

The straight line or ruler, is held in place and the airbrush is moved along the edge, then repeated.

Torn paper is used to create cloud effects.

15

Excercise Two

Try tearing paper and moving it around in different directions over the paper you are airbrushing, as seen in the photo above.

Excercise Three

Cut out a round or oval shape and try filling this area in, shading it more on the outer edges so that you create something that now looks three dimensional.

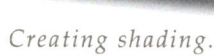

Creating shading.

Air Brushing, continued

When you have finished practicing, make sure that you run water through the airbrush until it is running clear. Don't allow any buildup of dye or paint in the airbrush as it will become clogged and will not work. Dyes tend to become quite rubbery once exposed to the air. The airbrush is made up of many small parts and will need cleaning properly from time to time. This should be done on a clear surface so that none of the parts become lost.

CHECK LIST FOR AIRBRUSHING

- Have plenty of paper towels or rags available.
- Cover tables with newspaper.
- Set the work up at a comfortable level.
- Begin practicing
- Hold the brush as you would a pen.
- Push the lever down for air
- Pull the lever back to paint
- The closer you are to the surface the finer the line or dot
- The further you are from the surface, the larger the area covered.
- Support the working hand with the other if this helps.

FIGURE 1
Clean and prepare your sewing machine.

TO GET READY to start your machine embroidery, make sure that your sewing machine is in good working order. If it hasn't been used for a while, you may want to give it a bit of a run first and clean any dust from the inside.

To prepare the machine for free-motion embroidery, remove the presser foot by unclipping or unscrewing it from the presser bar.

FIGURE 2
Removing the presser foot.

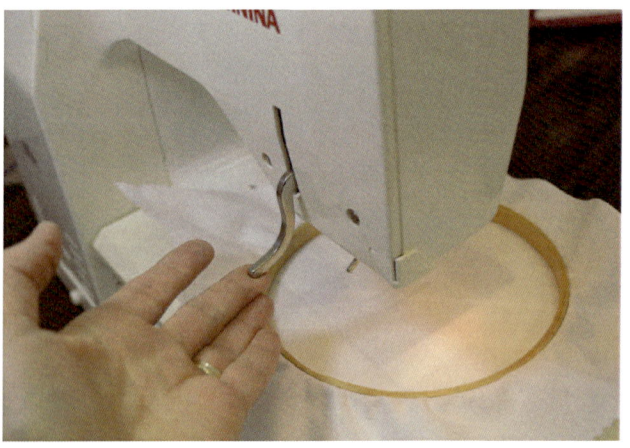

FIGURE 3
Make sure the lever, is in the down position.

Lower the feed dog. The feed dog guides the fabric along when you are sewing. There is usually a dial on the front of the machine for this. Also, lower the lever that has the feed dog on it. This is very important: if it is left in the up position, the thread may become tangled. It is also very easy to forget to do this.

Beginning Free Motion Embroidery

SOME MACHINES do not allow you to lower the feed dog, but these machines may have a raised plate to cover the feed dog. Once it has been lowered you are free to move your stretched fabric in any direction.

STRETCH YOUR PRACTICE FABRIC into an embroidery hoop. The fabric should be quite a bit larger than the hoop, which allows you to hold onto the fabric and pull it tightly. It is essential that the fabric is stretched as tight as a drum into the hoop. If the fabric is at all loose it can interfere with the stitches: They will not "catch" as easily as you move the hoop around underneath the needle.

The hoop will be placed on the sewing machine, with the fabric flat on the surface of the machine, underneath the needle. The best embroidery hoops actually have a little indentation for you to slide the hoop in easily under the needle.

When you begin to move the hoop around underneath the needle, try to keep the sewing machine running at a smooth and consistent speed. The more you practice, the easier it will become. Controlling the speed of the machine and the movement of the hoop may seem awkward initially. Experienced quilters will have no problem with this.

Begin the practice piece with different colors in the spool and the bobbin case. The reason for doing this is to see clearly the marks the top and the bottom threads are making. We will be changing the tension in the sewing machine to create different marks and textures.

Straight Stitch

LOWER the needle manually so that it catches the thread from underneath, that is, in the bobbin case. The needle will pull it up to the top and catch the stitch as you lift the needle. Then pull and hold the two ends of the thread out of the way.

FIGURE 4
The thread from below has been pulled to the top of the fabric, it is then held in place.

NEXT, start to move your hoop around in different directions. The examples in FIGURE 5 give you a few examples of the sort of movements you can make to feel comfortable.

FIGURE 5
Exercise 1. A simple straight stitch, used to create line and pattern.

Zigzag Stitch

TO CHANGE YOUR STITCH to zigzag, you will be using the buttons or knobs on the side of the sewing machine. See FIGURE 6.

The knob on my machine has numbers, the smallest number being the smallest width of the stitch. By changing the width from narrow to wide you can create many different patterns and textures and these can be changed depending on how you move the hoop in relation to how fast the sewing machine is going. The sample in FIGURE 7 shows some stitches to practice.

FIGURE 6
The dial allows you to change the width of the zigzag stitch.

FIGURE 7
Exercise 2. This sample shows the zigzag Stitch with width changes and direction changes.

IF YOU MOVE THE HOOP slowly while still keeping the speed of the machine fast, you will notice that you get a very dense solid satin stitch. Practice moving the hoop back and forth at different speeds and move it in large circular movements and smaller ones.

If you want to try making leaf shapes, you will need to hold the hoop with one hand while you turn the knob on the side of the machine, turning it back and fourth and decreasing and increasing the width of the zigzag stitch. (Some machines do not have knobs: they have a series of buttons that may or may not give you a smooth width increase.)

These sort of movements can allow you to create shapes that mimic leaves. As you experiment with the zigzag stitch, you will notice how versatile this stitch is and how it lends itself to mimicking a leaf design.

Whip Stitch

FOR THE WHIP STITCH, the thread on the top tension is made tighter than usual and the bottom tension is looser.

The stitch tension is regulated by a dial at the top of the sewing machine or at the front. Consult your manual if you are in doubt. Usually there are numbers on the dial. The tension becomes tighter the higher the number on the dial. When the number is lower it becomes looser. To alter the bobbin tension you may need to remove the bobbin case. In many machines the tension is controlled by a small screw in the bobbin case, which can be removed from the sewing machine. (Again, if you are in doubt refer to your manual.) This small screw regulates the tension of the flow of the thread. To loosen the tension of thread turn the screw counter-clockwise; to tighten it, turn it clockwise.

FIGURE 7
Loosen the screw of the bobbin case with a small screw driver.

These adjustments are very small and will require you to experiment a little to see what effects you can get by doing this. They will vary from sewing machine to sewing machine. Be careful not to overdo the loosening of the screw so that it pops out of the case and is lost.

PROCEED WITH THIS STITCH PRACTICE in the same way as you did for the straight and zigzag stitches. You will see in Figure 8 some examples of the marks made by moving your hoop in different directions, particularly in circles. You will notice that by moving your hoop in very small circles you will get the effect of tiny French knots. Larger circular movements create sea-anemone-like marks.

FIGURE 8
The example shows the thread color from the underneath. The thread is tighter on top and loose underneath.

FIGURE 9
The thread tension has been altered even more. The bobbin case has been further loosened.

The more you loosen the tension, the bigger the loops will be. The underneath thread will be pulled through the fabric to the top.

Practicing Your Stitching

NOW IT'S TIME to put to use the stitches you have learned. It is a good idea to do a sample on cotton. Keep it simple: you might want to use only black and grays on a simple white unpainted cotton. You will see that the marks you make are similar to pencil marks. Below the black and gray samples and on the next page there are more examples of free motion embroidery you may want to experiment with.

FIGURE 11
Using just greys you are able to practice shading.

FIGURE 10
Zigzag and straight stitches show the marks made are similar to pencil lines.

FIGURE 13
Fern created with a whip stitch.

FIGURE 12
The fern leaves are created from zigzag stitches.

FIGURE 14

FIGURE 15

FIGURE 16

FIGURE 17

FIGURE 20   FIGURE 21

FIGURE 18

FIGURE 22

FIGURE 23

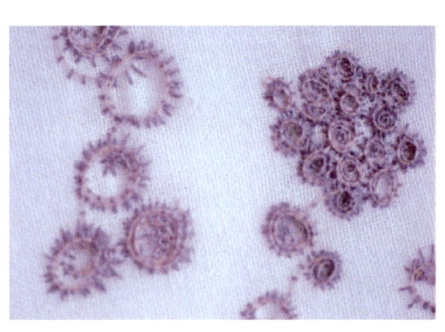
FIGURE 19

Beginning Free Motion Embroidery

FIGURE 14
Zigzag stitch in different widths creates the trunk and the branches.

FIGURE 15, 16
Zigzag stitch creates shrubs and leaves.

FIGURES 17, 18, 19
Show the effects you can create with a whip stitch.

FIGURE 20
Straight stitch using small movements creates the look of grass.

FIGURE 21
More straight stitching in different colors builds up texture.

FIGURE 22
Zigzag stitch moved a little more in different directions, creates a wilder looking shrub.

FIGURE 23
Zigzag stitch where the width changes from wide to narrow, creates plant or leaf marks.

Machine Embroidery Check List

- Make sure the sewing machine is in working order and practice regular sewing before you begin free motion.
- Thread the machine and bobbin case correctly.
- Make sure your needle is sharp.
- Remove the presser foot.
- Lower the feed dog.
- Make sure the lever that usually lowers the presser foot is in the down position.
- Keep your fingers away from the unguarded needle. Use the darning foot if it makes you more comfortable.
- Make sure the fabric is stretched as tight as a drum in the embroidery hoop.
- Draw the bobbin thread up to the top of the fabric manually.
- Hold the top and bottom thread in place before you begin stitching.
- Adjust your tension to the stitch you are wanting.
- Move the hoop underneath the needle slowly, avoiding jerky movements that might break your threads.

FIGURE 1
Source Photo:
A Pathway in Mendon.

Choose your subject

- PREPARE the silk by ironing it to remove creases before airbrushing with the fabric dyes.

- MEASURE the size of the stretcher frame and allow the fabric to be a little larger than your frame.

- TO CUT A STRAIGHT EDGE, take a tiny thread from the edge of the silk and pull at it. This will give you a guide to cut a straight edge.

FIGURE 2
Pulling thread.

- STRETCH THE SILK onto a wooden frame using silk pins. Begin at one corner and stretch the silk to each of the four corners and continue around the frame.

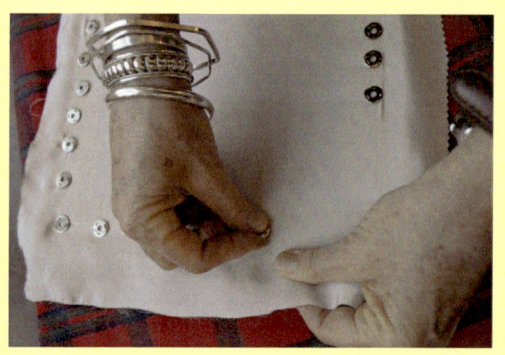

FIGURE 3
Pinning silk.

Beginning the First Project

Making a Stencil

- Cut the blotting paper to the same size as the wooden stretcher frame.

- Measure and draw a ruled line of approximately two inches along the sides of the paper as in FIGURE 4.

- Take your design and trace with a pencil the simple, basic lines of your landscape as in FIGURE 5.

- Transfer these marks onto your blotting paper, using the tracing paper as in FIGURE 6.

FIGURE 4

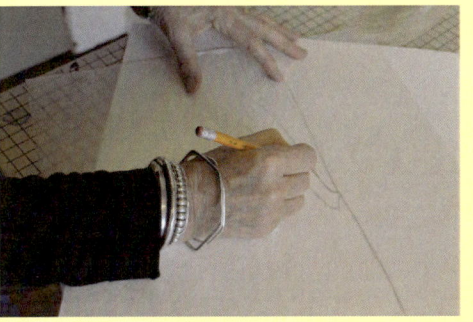 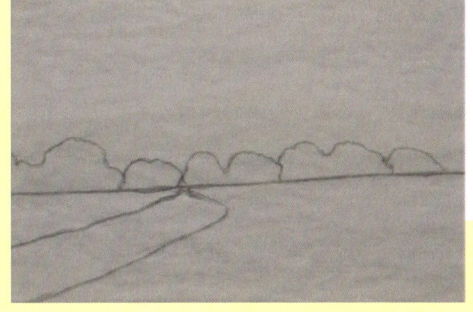

FIGURES 5 AND 6

- Take the blotting paper and put it on a quilter's table or a surface you can cut on. Then with your X-acto knife begin to cut along where the skyline touches the borders of the paper. Continue down along the side until you get to the horizon, then cut along the horizon. FIGURE 7

- Stop at the border, leaving a flap that can be folded back as you begin to airbrush. FIGURE 8

- Now do the same for the landscape and pathway, again leaving one side attached.

FIGURE 9   FIGURE 10

You now have a stencil for the background for your thread painting!

Spraying Your Background

- **FIGURE 11**
  Place the stencil onto your stretched silk and place the frame on an easel. Begin to airbrush the sky as shown in the photo on page 16.

- **FIGURE 12**
  The silk has now been airbrushed and the stencil removed.

- When the background is prepared, iron the silk on the reverse side of the airbrushing to fix the dye or the paint.

- Stretch the fabric into the embroidery hoop with a cotton backing.

FIGURE 13
Shows treated fabric ready for stretching into the hoop.

FIGURE 14
Shows the cotton fabric backing.

FIGURE 15
The fabric is stretched tightly into a hoop with a cotton backing.

Beginning the First Project, continued

FIGURE 16
Choose the colors you plan to work with based on the photograph.

FIGURE 17
Dark green threads are worked in a zigzag stitch to begin the lower part of the shrubs.

- By referring to your photograph, begin to work on the area that is the most distant. In this design I have not included the very distant trees; I have begun with the shrubs at the horizon.

- Using the zigzag stitch with the loosened tension, put down dark green for the first color. The next color used is a slightly lighter green to begin the shading of the shrubs on the side where the light is coming from.

FIGURE 18
Beginning to move forward, I choose a sand colored thread and use a straight stitch for the grasses.

- Once the shrubs are complete, the ground covering just in front of the shrubs is filled in using two colors, beige on the spool and yellow in the bobbin. I have used the straight stitch, the lower tension remains loosened.

FIGURE 19
The shrubs are completed, I begin to work on the pathway.

- Working forward I have begun to change the colors, gradually moving into green shades, as seen in the original photograph, At the same time I am elongating the stitch to create the effect of grasses.

FIGURE 20
The Pathway has been worked using a straight stitch working horizonally. The grasses at the forefront are worked with the straight stitch, with longer lines.

- As I progress to the foreground I use a mixture of zigzag and straight stiches to create the feeling of grasses, leaves and wild flowers.

- The work is finished and ready for mounting and presentation.

FIGURE 22
Completed work. Flowers have been created using both zigzag stitch and a straight stitch.

Beginning the First Project, continued

FIGURE 21
Photograph shows close up view of the stitches. These are a combination of straight stitches; the milkweed is worked in zigzag stitches.

SOURCE PHOTO: Trees in Mendon

Repeating the same process I used in the first project, I have scanned the photograph and enlarged it before printing. I have then simplified the image and drawn my lines to make the stencil.

FIGURE 1
The image from the source photograph has been simplified to a few lines.

FIGURE 2
Cutting the Stencil.

Trace the lines on to your blotting paper and with the X-acto knife cut out a stencil. The processes from the first project are then repeated. The silk is ironed and stretched using silk thumb tacks onto a stretching frame, the stencil set in place and the background airbrushed.

FIGURE 3 *Stretched and airbrushed, the background is ready.*

FIGURE 4 *The Background is ready for the embroidery. It has been ironed and placed in a hoop.*

Second Project, Autumn Trees

First I begin to work with a dark green thread at the lowest part of the shrubs. I use a zigzag stitch with the bobbin tension loose and the top tension is tighter. This creates depth and texture.

FIGURE 5
A combination of different size zigzag stitches are used for the trees.

To create the shading I choose threads from a variety of lighter shades of greens, incorporating yellows and soft rusts sometimes. The threads are often different colors in the bobbin case and on the spool, this creates a more painterly look. The tree trunks in this piece are created by using a wider zigzag stitch at the bottom part of the trunk and gradually making it narrower as I progress to the top. The branches are worked with a mix of different widths of zigzag stitch.

FIGURE 6 *Work in progress.*

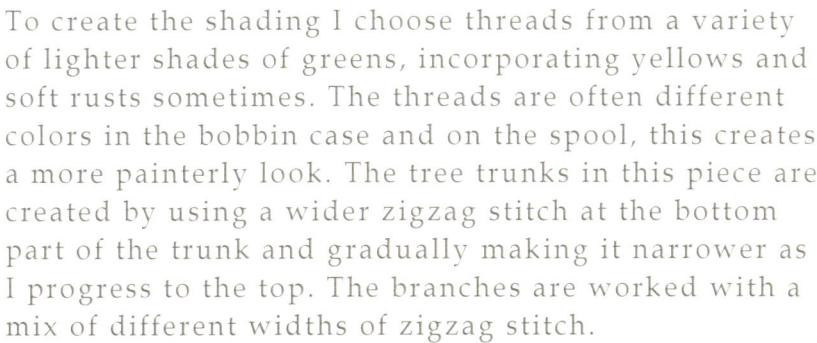

FIGURE 7
Completed piece.

FIGURE 8
Close up showing the detail of straight stitches in the foreground.

Second Project, Autumn Trees, continued

FIGURE 9
Close up of the Autumn Trees.

FIGURE 10
Completed Thread Painting of Autumn Trees, stretched and matted.

Eve Botelho
FINISHED WORK
A Drive in the Fall

Eve Botelho
FINISHED WORK
A Field in Mendon

Eve Botelho, FINISHED WORK, *Cherry Trees in Highland Park*

Eve Botelho , FINISHED WORK, *A Walk in Corbett's Glen*

Eve Botelho, FINISHED WORK, *Milkweed in Mendon*

Third Project

A Field in Mendon

FIGURE 1 *Source photo of a farm field.*

FIGURE 2
Airbrushed background and the beginning stitches.

FIGURE 3
The shading of the trees in the background is put down before the grasses in the foreground.

FIGURE 4
The trees are finished, I am beginning the grass in straight stitch.

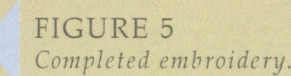

FIGURE 6
Close up of fininished work.

FIGURE 5
Completed embroidery.

41

Eve Botelho, FINISHED WORK, *Gentle Chaos*

Goldenrods
Fourth Project

FIGURE 1 *Source photo, Field of Goldenrod.*

FIGURE 2 *Simple background of airbrushed silk.*

FIGURE 3
The shading of the trees in the background is put down before the grasses in the foreground.

FIGURE 4
Then the grasses and other foreground details are added.

FIGURE 5
Almost finshed and ready for stretching.

FIGURE 6, *The finished work.*

Eve Botelho, FINISHED WORK, DETAIL, *Formal Garden*

Eve Botelho, FINISHED WORK, *Dappled Sunlight at Corbett's Glen*

Conclusion

Presentation

Once you have a completed the piece it is now ready for **PRESENTATION**.

The work may have become a little distorted, because of the varying amounts of stitching on the background of some areas and you may have other areas that have little or no stitching.

It will be necessary to stretch the work carefully and tightly. You should end up with a taut and flat image. This is achieved by using archival foam core. Archival materials are acid free and will prevent discoloration in the work.

Cut the foam core a little larger than the completed thread painting, to allow the edges of the fabric to wrap around the board.

Hold the fabric firmly and put the silk pins through the fabric into the side of the board. Silk pins are very smooth and will not tear the fabric.

FIGURE 1
Finished work ready to be stretched.

FIGURE 2
Cut the foam core slightly larger than the finished piece.

FIGURE 3
The work is stretched over acid free foam core, using silk pins.

FIGURE 4
Continue to put pins all the way around the foam core making sure the fabric is pulled taut.

FIGURE 5
If you like, you can lace the back of the fabric and then remove the pins.

Ideally you will want to keep the work protected under glass and framed. Presentation is an important and integral part of the process.

I choose the color of the mat board carefully, coordinating or complementing the color with the overall color of the thread painting. Personal taste will be the basis for the selection of your frame, though it is good to check that there is enough depth in the frame for the stretched work, two or three mat boards, the glass and the backing. If you take the work to a professional, they will help with this.

FIGURE 6
Matted with painted boarders.

Presentation
CONTINUED

I sometimes enjoy extending the landscapes onto the mat board and may paint and airbrush on a white mat board.

Here are some examples of the presentation with the mat board airbrushed and then detail added with acrylics and watercolors. The image extends onto the mat board.

FIGURE 7 ▲

FIGURE 8 ▼

Close up of painted border and the detail of stitches.

FIGURE 9 ▶

Favorite Framing styles

Resources

DHARMA TRADING CO.
www.dharmatrading.com
1805 South McDowell Boulevard Ext.
Petaulma, CA 94954
Toll free 800-283-0390
E-mail service@dharmatrading.com

UNCOMMON THREAD
www.uncommonthread.com
2342C Ebenezer Road
Rock Hill, SC 29732
Toll free 866-829-7235 or 803-327-8866
E-mail speedstitch@comporium.net

BLICK ART MATERIALS
www.dickblick.com
3424 Cosby Place
Charlotte, NC 28205
Toll free 800-828-4548
E-mail eve@evebotelho.com

Acknowledgments

I am grateful to the following people for the help I have had with this book: my friends, who have brought their professional eye to the project, particularly Denise Kovnat and Pat Aslin; my daughters, Sara, for her honest and helpful criticism and Anna, for being a cheerleader; and my husband, Rick, for his support. I would also like to thank my book designer, Katherine Denison, for doing a smashing job; Brittany McCulloch, for the final edit; and my photographers, Stephanie Quinones Millet and Alene Pierro.

www.ingramcontent.com/pod-product-compliance
Lightning Source LLC
Chambersburg PA
CBRC090837010526
44118CB00007B/236